DIVE WITHIN

Poetry on Fighting Lymphoma and
Mental Health plus Novella-in-Verse

Christina Vourcos

Independently Published

To Dr. Robb Jackson,

Thank you for teaching me to write poetry, but most of all, teaching me that poetry is therapeutic. You allowed my words to not be constrained by rules. You taught me to survive. I wouldn't be a poet and survive Lymphoma without you and everything you taught me years ago. Your presence lives on through all your students.

Also to mi abuelita Rosie Vourcos,
I miss you so much. Thank you for all your love, but also showing me how to get through the difficult moments in life. You fought lymphoma and became a survivor before I lost you, but your presence helped me through my fight with lymphoma and so much more.

CONTENTS

PART ONE: THE FIGHT

I'm The Book Cover

How does one start the next book
Without looking at the first?

So much has changed now
Evolved into lasting trauma
We want to grow out of

From South Texas to New York
I've written from the heart
No matter how much precise
measure will never be perfect

Only the beautiful, messy recipe
made with an understanding
That nothing can be perfect
All you can do is your best

Even if you're fighting battles
Within that, only medical exams
And counseling sessions that
Doctors, nurses, and counselors
Can truly see, but you try anyway

It's time to start a new volume
Let's see what comes our way

SURREALISTIC ANSWERS

Looking at a photograph forever
You'll never find me; chase me
When you can feel what you can't see
The clouds fall to the ground surrounding me

Your mind keeps thinking of words
The water on the beach with a unique taste
Sound of force coming down far through the sky
The rain with a specific tune to dance to

The past that haunts through the night
You'll find the world can be your oyster
With a pearl inside, but it's an adventure
That you must partake

FIGHTING WITHIN THE BLOOD

When something within the blood changes
It can be hard to see, even through a microscope
It can't be confirmed without a cut in the skin
Blood can be drawn, but it's just not enough

Several cut samples might be needed
Until they can make their conclusions
But you might already be too late
If only they had taken the symptoms as a sign
One cannot go back in time or know for sure

Everyone is trying their best to find the cure
For now, you have to accept the treatment
That will affect the good just as much as the bad
Only hope that time will go by fast
All will be resolved for survivorship

Because no matter how much you see it
Cancer isn't always a death sentence
Especially if you have a blood cancer,
Like lymphoma, like the poet,
As long as you keep fighting forward
You'll learn you're stronger, body and mind.

REST DAYS

No matter what you have
You'll need rest days
It's hard to do, but you must
Otherwise, your body
Will make the decision

Listen to what you feel
It's just as important as logic
You can overcome when you rest
Take some time to relax
Your recovery needs it

The list needs to be cut
Eventually, it will work out
Time to meditate and self-care
The rollercoaster of chemo will be
Slightly better with time

CHEMO SUPERPOWERS

Don't tell me it isn't possible
Magic is possible if you look for it
So can superpowers be
Is it a secret that I hope?

Everyone knows that I'm a nerd
We love to imagine we can be anything
Isn't that what makes a writer too?
Maybe I've had superpowers
But I didn't know it; the strength within

The creativity of one's mind
The compassion to make a difference
Proud to be a nerd before and after

It's still fun to imagine the superpowers:
Quick to read amazing stories and poems
Provide support always one hundred percent
Star power to head anywhere quickly
Get everything I want and need done...

Wait, it's starting to get real again
Time to go back to my imagination

MEDITATION

Self-care is meditation with music
Soothing music in the background
As you let your mind rest of thought
Focus on your breath in and out

It seems simple, but sometimes it's not
Your mind will wander away
You'll have to start again
Rocking back and forth in a chair
Breathing in and out with focus

It's a spa for your mind
A different kind of rest that
Can be prayer if you decide
It doesn't have to be prayer
Especially when your mind needs
Rest after a long day or session of chemo

Allow the music to massage your mind
Maybe meditation can be a massage
Your mind and body aligned
Take some time to rest
Self-care will do you good
Then you can be you

A DIFFERENT HAT

My chemo journey was mine
I wasn't going to accept another path
No shaving my hair for a bald head
If I would lose my hair, it would
There were scarfs and wraps

They weren't me, no matter the color
Others could choose that path, but not me
Hats have always been me
So finding one for my journey
Made sense it would feel right to me

Soft corduroy black with a touch of brown
Felt perfectly Greek to me
No matter the pain or struggle
In this journey, I would be me
A simple cap for some, but normality
As I put on a different hat

PROJECTS

All the things that I need to do
All the things that I want to do
A growing list of ever-changing

Projects I need to start
Projects I want to start
Projects I have started
Waiting to be finished

So much pushed aside
No matter how I try to move
Forward doesn't seem ahead
Always behind, never on time
Told that I need rest but don't know how

My mind is racing with all the things left
What if time runs out? Left undone
Projects you're waiting on
At least I hope you are

BLUE MESSAGE

If I could write a physical letter,
The envelope would be blue
Not for the sadness that I would say
Or the memories of a painful time

It would be blue because it's true
Calm that flows within me
Knowing that I've gone through
More than I ever expected to

Blue because it's the water
That I'm drawn to as the waves
Blue because you are more super
Than you can ever imagine

You'll know this message is for
You because it's me in the future

SEA DREAMS

My perfect place is by the beach
Where the clouds are gray above
But no rain in sight, only cool temps

I can grab a book at the nearby store
Or read one that I bring along
I can sit in a wooden rocking chair
View the waves crashing on the shore

I can walk along the beach with
A camera in hand to capture it
I go now more than before

I still dream of going back for more
It's all part of my sea dreams

OVERHEARD THOUGHTS

"¿Escuchaste lo que pasó?"
They were at it again
Talking about others
Thinking no one would know

They can't imagine I know
The language they use
To speak of others so
No one will know

"Ella no es tan buena como dice."
Are they talking about me?
They aren't saying my name
Who else could it be?
If it's my work, I try my best
I know that I'm not perfect

"¿Ves cómo se ve?"
What is wrong with me?
I can't afford to get new clothes
Why would I when I could
Use that money for books

"No confío en ella."
They don't even know me
I don't care what they say
Estoy tratando lo mejor que puedo.

DEAR POEM

I want to write you
My mind won't clear
The fog looming through
It doesn't make sense

Writing is my passion
When I write poetry
A poem, like you,
It gives me a chance
To reflect on my thoughts

It isn't easy with my mind
Directing what I can do
It's not all my mind
But my body too
When everything drains
I'm half of who I am

What can I do to write?
Do you have any ideas?
What do you want to say?
My mind and body tell me
That I should wait

Focus on something else
Like reading a while
Or taking some notes
Can you help me write
So you can come alive?

WAITING FOR NEWS

It's always hard to wait for news
Especially for the impatient
From one day to several days
It could even be weeks or months

You never know what would happen
Maybe something got lost or not enough
Was done to make sure it was ready
In many cases, it's out of your control

They take what they think they need
It might not be enough, but who knows
What if the news isn't what you expect?
At least there's knowledge to work with

The unknown or unexpected is what's
Difficult to work with until it happens
You figure it out as best as you can
You need to know to ease your mind

BEACH TIME

It's a quick mini-vacation
Only 30 minutes by car
A bit farther than most
But the park is worth it

At the right times
The beach is all for you
No matter what the time
The beach is there for you
The waves heading to the shore
The sand touching your feet
Taking some time to breathe

Gives you time to reset
With those you care most
It's just what you need
Especially after treatments
With stressful side effects

No time to worry or work
Just take a photo or more
You walk along the water
It sets you back right
All with some
Beach time

NOTES

Don't forget something
Sometimes it's hard to keep up
With the little details, unlike
The big plot points of a story
That's why it helps to take notes

It's hard to remember things
When you go through chemo
Your brain gets foggy with meds
It doesn't seem to be working
So you take notes to make sure

Sometimes you need someone
Taking notes so words aren't hard
But usually, you take notes
For yourself because it helps
Clear the thoughts in your mind

YES, MAYBE, NO

Yes, I want to write
Maybe you can, says the mind
So why am I not writing
No, you cannot write today
Maybe I need to change things

Yes, change could help
I'll experiment to see
Maybe that will work
Am I seeing results?

Yes, a bit here, keep going
Is it enough what I share?
Maybe, I'm not sure exactly
No, I need to know now
It's going to take time
Yes, I know that it will

Maybe you can write today
Yes, I will write something
No, that won't work out
Maybe I need time to rest
Yes, let me rest a bit more
Maybe I'll write it down
Yes, you'll write it now

FEARSOME LOOP

One weekend after a treatment
It wasn't the usual chemo side effects
Now it's long nights with no sleep
While I caught up with sleep one day
The rest was not coming enough

By the weekend, emotions bubbled
That kept me up through midnight
I couldn't stop thinking and repeating
I couldn't stop thinking and repeating
The actions didn't make sense

It felt like a religious experience
That others couldn't understand
My hands moved as I knew
American Sign Language perfectly
But it still didn't make sense

I couldn't stop speaking strange
Thoughts out loud until
I was treated for a night
And a day in the hospital
It still scares me to this day

I know now the extra value
Keeping up self-care
As best as you can or
With a bit of help
I made it out of the
Fearsome loop

STRANGE DAYS

I would get blood drawn
The day before to get ready

I would wear a special shirt
Just to access my chemo port
If the port was acting up
My day would start with pain
After the medicine would
Wear me down and change

The days after with side effects
Now chemo is done, but it's not
Over, I've got radiation now
I don't need to take days off

Short sessions are at midday
In between my workdays
And feet pulling my shoulders down
A mask pushes down on my face

I keep breathing as the machine
Goes by my neck with radiation
A mask that feels strange until
I pretend I'm a superhero

After a bit of time
I'm done until another day
Fatigue continues from
Chemo to Radiation
Now I count the days to go

RADIATION ANXIETY

The days after the CT scans
I had to wait for the plans
People deciding my Radiation
I needed to know my prescription

I'm impatient, I needed to know
I wanted to get started already
No one seemed to understand
Why was I rushed to start?

I needed to know my schedule
What I would do every day
I can work with knowledge
I need a set daily schedule

I need to know my future
That things will be clearer
As radiation starts and ends

I'll know how much with effect:
The growing fatigue from
All over my body and mind
The increasing pain and dryness
Through my neck, throat, and mouth

Even after the treatments end,
There are still side effects that
Could extend for weeks
It all lingers in my mind
I can work with knowledge

HER 'HURT' SELF

She was tired of everything
She was annoyed by imperfections
She was annoyed by interceptions
Where her parents didn't understand
Or other family or friends throughout

She was too tired to keep going each day
Always plenty of issues to deal with
Nothing seemed to be solved yesterday
She wanted changes they could see
Others kept saying she could do better

Then it went deeper, something changed
Her body couldn't control the disease
She was tired all the time no one knew
It was like an endless pull into deep water
But she was always trying to pull up

She was in pain in ways that words left her
Nothing seemed to be going right
The roller coaster of the treatments
Left her, unlike her past self, her hurt
It took her to slow down to love herself

Everyone can't imagine going less
It must be done today, no rest
If she did, she was a failure
Why would they want her
They wanted someone
That wasn't her

HER 'LOWEST' SELF

She knew that she didn't deserve
The ways she was being treated
They didn't respect her and when
She raised her voice for change

It didn't seem to work, but she kept
At it because how dare they treat her
Different because she was younger
They thought they could direct her
They thought she would let them be
She didn't deserve to be disrespected
From students, parents, co-workers

She had to break down to choose herself
What if that brokenness led to worse
What if that changed her body to create
An increase in disease within
The stress came way before the broken

After even more stress from the unknown
Where would she be if this didn't happen
Would she not have to fight a disease?
Would she not have learned her broken past?
Would she not have found strength within?
Would she not become a fighter for justice?
Her lowest self needed to grow within
To change what needed to be

HER 'HIGHEST' SELF

She has learned that people will hurt
Through words and actions, but
Forgiveness is greater than pain
She has taken what she has learned
With hope that it will inspire change
From education, writing, and life
Even fighting against disease

It's all part of the struggle within
She felt the world didn't know how
Their actions changed her from the start
Every step now she takes is to reset
The actions that others have done
She won't let hurtful words stay
She will focus on what's next today

The challenge is finding one's self
At the finish line with fog ahead
She is the adult caring for herself
Self-love was something not taught
Faith as it's seen as selfishness
Therefore she had to learn elsewhere

Now it's up to her to change fate
And the world to realize what
She deserves what we all deserve
Finding a way to care about ourselves
So we hurt less and love more

IDENTIFYING IDENTITY

I've always loved Romance in stories
It always seemed like someday
I would find the one that made me
Feel special and be a partner for life
But I can't find someone at my level

When I thought it would work
My heart would accept unrequited
The ones that were interested in kissing
Every time it repelling as touch
Was it because I wasn't in love?
Or was it something else?

No, I was interested in male leads
At least the ones in good stories
Maybe they led to expectations
But I knew they existed in real life
Just no one that I could find

So I focus now self-care
Working words with possibilities
Falling in love with characters
Explore their lives along with mine
All I need to be is a writer

CRAVING/DISTASTE

They were always my sweet
Rice Krispies made just for me
Now they were wrapped to eat
As I struggled to get through chemo

Whatever food I found that I craved
I was getting through the worst
How could I be denied a craving?

With very few taste changes and
Only a few moments of lack of appetite
It was the saving grace during those days

Soon things would change with the pain
Instead of throughout my body
The radiation treatments on my neck
It completely changed what I could eat

From the distaste of favorite foods
To unfamiliar taste of everything
The food looked good, but nothing
Worked as it should to go down

The drying of my mouth added
Another layer to the pain is unexplained
Water wasn't enough for my thirst
Sprite, no 7Up, was the comfort needed
From craving to distaste to comfort

With rest, it will all reset
Nothing will match the lost taste

SLOWING THE PAIN

I thought losing an unrequited love was hard
Until I started fighting lymphoma
Radiation was what I expected chemo to be
Slowly gradually growing in pain and fatigue

Chemotherapy was the roller coaster
Radiation therapy was the worst sunburn
I couldn't control the pain with Chemo
I couldn't control the pain with Radiation

I wish I could say the bitter pain has left
Even after treatments are over, the pain lingers
Throat swollen and dry like a sore throat
But it's lasted so much longer than normal

It's hard to swallow almost everything
Let's not talk about the taste changes
Writing has always been my voice
Although singing has from time to time
But now my raspy voice adds to the pain

The doctor says it will gradually go away
All the side effects that I've had, but
It seems so far away from now
All I can do is limit my voice out loud
Thankfully the words are still here

INDEX OF THE MIND

I scan through my memory files
If I could walk through the files
They would be like walking through
A library filled with books from top to bottom

Why am I looking through the past files?
It could be a way to break generational trauma
If my mind could make a Genogram
A family tree to explore and understand
How the past shaped me, and eventually
Heal me from the invisible wounds within

One delirium episode after a round of Chemo
Made a breakthrough of what has held me back
A long-winded fear of losing unexpected control
Where did it come from you may wonder?
Could it be from the moves to different places
Could it be from moments I can't let go?
Could it be from the expectations held?

Or is it just that I fear what will hurt me?
What could be worse than fighting cancer?
Could it be losing oneself beyond recognition?
Could it be the future not set in stone?
Could it be not knowing who will be there?

I have care now, but what if it isn't later
I understand that I'm lucky from others
What can I do to improve this anxiety?

NO TURNING BACK

The words can not be returned
People have read what matters most
No matter what someone says it isn't enough

Where could I have made those changes?
Isn't it possible that you need to see my growth?
There's no turning back from these words

I know I can improve with every word
Please keep giving me time as I write
I don't want to go back and change
Every word was written down and read

Maybe they were meant to be that way
Evidence of my growing creativity
Evidence that I've learned languages
There's no turning back, only forward

HEALTH REVIEW

Not everyone would fear a health review
It's just a moment to check what's there
I'm still young and healthy by the eye

With a medical scan, they can see within
Years before they noticed a concern
Never followed through until the worse
Now the latest scans have been good
After they found the worst months ago

But now that I'm in recovery, it's looming
I don't want to go through the pain again
Something I didn't even know to prevent
They can only test to see how I am

There's no preventative measure with
Unexplainable cause of cancer,
Lymphoma turned in the lymph nodes,
Flowing through lymph vessels and blood
Even worse when it goes to the bone marrow

They can do all they can with treatments
You and I can not prevent the return
Only continue to stop this villain in its tracks
Through these health reviews through the years

FUTURE RECOGNITION

Recognition isn't the same as fame
Heroes want to be recognized
For their good works and actions
They don't want attention like fame

Although there might be a few
That want attention, it's human,
Or they lack some of it somewhere

While we might not see superheroes
In our real lives, heroes show up
They do it to help others, but
There's still a cost involved

Some are quick to say certain careers
Those people are heroes, not understanding
They say it in admiration, but is it?

Some are quick to say heroes are all about
Making a difference, that is true, but
It can lead to people thinking they don't
Deserve support to survive

They want heroes to sacrifice
Because isn't recognition enough
Sometimes it can be, but never enough

Nurses, teachers, and writers want to be recognized
They usually don't want overwhelming fame
They want to be able to keep doing their passion

A PERFECT BIRTHDAY

If I could have a perfect birthday
With no concern of cost for that day
I would take a trip to visit New York
Then travel to an island in Greece

I would see my friends far away
See once again Broadway
I would go on my way
To see my family roots

I would head to Lesvos
To learn more than before
Where my family came from
With the magic inspiration

To write a story on page
And within me with moments
Made by people I meet
Maybe even fall in love

If I had a perfect birthday
I would spend it at the beach
And a water park with slides
Allowing myself to be me

No stress of work looming
No worries about finishing
The next written project

Just allowing my passions
To flow through me

PART TWO: RECOVERY

I'm Looking For Creativity

I put a lot of pressure on myself
I want to get back to my normal
Where I could write more than now
I'm reminded that I'm recovering

Yet I still look for creativity
I miss the feeling of writing
With a focus on the project
Seeing each chapter completed

Yet I still look for creativity
I want to write a poem each day
It's something that I know I can do
Even something small seems drowning

Yet I still look for creativity
I know writing will raise my mood
Yet no matter my desire, I don't know
If I can find the words for the page

Yet I still look for creativity
I try to read for inspiration
It makes me miss writing more
While I struggle to focus on words

I'm looking for creativity
Can you help me find her?

SHE'S LOOKING FOR CREATIVITY

She puts a lot of pressure on herself
All to get back to some form of "normal"
Where she thinks she can write more
No matter how "recovery" is repeated

Yet she still looks for creativity
Missing the feeling of writing
With a focus on the flow
Until each chapter completed

Yet she still looks for creativity
With an expectation that
Writing a poem each day is possible
But something small seems drowning

Yet she still looks for creativity
With the idea that writing will raise
The mood as it has done in the past
Yet no matter the desire, the body
Won't let her find the words

Yet she still looks for creativity
Through each book read
But it makes her miss writing more
While the mind struggles to focus

She is looking for creativity
Will she be able to write now?

FINDING WAYS TO COPE

Recovery should be like a vacation
Time to relax and rest, body and mind
Recovery isn't easy when you're not well
It isn't easy when it seems like you're better

Recovery should be time to cope
With everything the lymphoma fight
Takes you through body and soul
But it's like an aspect that can't be seen

What others expect, what you expect
It's faster than what is possible
Pushing yourself forward more
Won't always help, but self-care will

You know that it will take time
You just don't have the patience
So you try to find something
Anything that will move you
Towards progress to cope

Even though you need rest

FUTURE POWER

I wish I could have future power
I could see what is ahead
So I could find out what I do

If I knew, I could plan ahead
Or change course if needed
But what if that isn't enough

Why do I need to know?
I don't have the patience
Even if I knew what's ahead

What if it's not enough?
What if there's still some left
Within the waves out of reach

It's like reading the end first
Why can't I focus on the now?
Worried about the future and past

What if I haven't resolved the past,
Does it change the actions for the future?
What will I truly gain from knowing?

I can't rest enough now
I'll struggle even more with power
Desire pushes me forward
It's the power of the future

MEMORIAS DE AMISTAD

If only friendships could be easy
They seemed to be in memories
You could meet someone to spend time

Now friends are far away or busy
If they still want to speak with you
In fighting lymphoma, it changes

It makes you wonder what you have
Even though death isn't near
The struggle still reminds you

Have you done enough?
You already have the fight
Why do you need to worry?

Memories of distant friends
Along with the support online
Confuses your mind and heart

Would you find life better?
If you did something different?
Or will you be left with recuerdos?

LA PLAYA DEL PASADO

Puedo imaginar la playa del pasado
Mi familia went to the beach in late summer
A few hours away in South Padre Island
Near Brownsville and the Border

We would pack up the car for the day
Including what we needed for lunch
All I remembered the most was the chips
With the side of orange soda

Mi mami y abuelita worried about me
Sunscreen and limited time in the sun
Never too far into the water, near the sand
Watching on seeing what I was doing

Mi abuelo enjoying the moment
While mi papi near me in the water
I never wanted to leave by the end
Staying for a few nights was rare

La pequeña dreamed of living there
It would be years when her sueño
Would come true near another playa

CALLING THE MUSE

Muse, will you please stay?
You keep my mind ready
For all kinds of inspiration

You and your work seem elusive
If it's something you need
What shall I provide?

I come to the page willing
Many things hold me back
Especially with the most creative

Muse, don't forget me!
I'm trying all that I can
The process seems slow

The words of the mind
Seem far from my reach
I know that you can help

If I write in verse
I can break the curse
At least a little bit
Are you answering?

MISSING ROMANCE

It's hard to find someone
That matches your level
Yet you miss the excitement
Of finding someone charming

When you're stuck inside
It seems the solution is online
Even the World Wide Web
Holds unexpected traps

Romance stories like fantasy
Magic that seems out of reach
You can only live through it
From the pages to the screen

How do you write it down
When your heart isn't there
Your mind is somewhere else
Your body fatigued from it all

Where is Romance hiding?
Do you even want to find it?
Or do you just want to write?
It is all out of your control

A SHIP IN THE NIGHT

Your mind travels through the night
On a ship of waves in the Gulf of Mexico
The ship depth files of deeply held past
Your heart beside like a broken shipwreck

The night sky guides you through
Whales in the ocean meeting the stars
Starfish scattered on the ocean floor
Seaweed sent as messages by the sea

The strong scent of sea salt looms
Meditation for your soulful curiosity
In the dark time for reading
The ocean is like an open book

Raw oysters flavor your thoughts
As they were the memory of the lost
Fearful of the broken glass scattered
On the ship's hidden kitchen floor

The waves slowly fade into flattened space
You know below the surface someone left trash
The negative comments destroying the depths
Constellations of thoughts connecting
Waves of radio signals call out
A midnight zone of silence

As a storm rushes towards the ship
Vibration all through the body
As the current takes place within

NATURE'S REQUEST

Scorching evaporation of a once-dive
into the channel of summertime
Lake water waiting for locals and visitors
to take the plunge but they only stand by

Imagining stories of those encounters towards
adventure, lake water filled to the rim
where young people jump in the final days
of summer alongside their crushes

Now heat caused by our own devices
changed the dynamics of stories and landscape
Like an illness that could have been prevented

Here it's hard to imagine uncontrollable
scorching fires warping the lands driving away
those who lived there for years

One wonders what kind of actions
would be taken if more believed in
making things better than what has been given
Earth's cure and recovery can't come soon enough

UNA FRUTA FAVORITA

La papaya Mexicana
Con una estrella naturaleza
Dulce con limón y especias
Listo para comer en tu plato
Conexión con mi cultura
Como granada y mi otra cultura

La papaya mexicana es saludable
Pero puede ser postre durante el día
No importa como lo comas
Pero eso es mi favorito

Yo estoy lista para que ayuda
Sentir más mejor ahora

DAILY STRUGGLE

Every day is a constant struggle
From almost every aspect I'm cured
People can't see that it's still difficult
I can't be on demand all the time
It's not my choice, my body decides

I'm in recovery, but work can't see it
I must be flexible as it was given to me
As if flexibility was a reward
That must be returned quickly
Just like the emails that must
Be responded to as soon as possible
Or you're late and irresponsible

I understand that we're working with less
I'm also working with less,
But it doesn't seem to matter
I'm told I'm asking for too much
As if it's unreasonable yet
When I've gone through the worst
Somehow kept putting in the hours

I did it more than just for the money
I wanted to make sure we weren't behind
Is it because I want to be seen well?
Is it hard because I care too much?
Every day I feel like I'm breaking
I wish I could afford to work for myself

LANGUAGE WAVES

Learning a language never has been easy
Until finding something technological
Each day becomes an opportunity

You can learn as you go, like a game
With levels to reach towards
Different languages to choose

Like the waves of the ocean
You have to be consistent
Each day learning something

The more you learn, the more
You understand the language
You've always wanted to know

The languages of your heritage
Connect with the most, especially
If you couldn't learn from your ancestors

The connection between you
And others that allow you to be
Part of your communities

You test the waters when you write
You want to be at your best
So they'll know your past

UNWELL & UNSETTLED

The scans were scheduled to come
It should be something routine
It made everything feel unsettled

Something felt off with my body
My mind was just as concerned
I couldn't understand what it was

The stomach didn't keep anything down
Even if I didn't eat anything for hours
Fluids would go up and fall everywhere

Was I sick? Did the lymphoma return?
Did I have another cancer? Questions remain
I wanted the unwell feelings to go away

I needed reassurance and answers
But they were making me wait
Even then I had to act okay

What if they would make me wait
Days or weeks longer because
They didn't want me sick

I may never know as good news
Settled in and sickness drifted
Was it anxiety or temporary sickness?

SCANS OF GOOD NEWS

The reports were coming in
The doctor would soon see me
I was ready for some good news

I knew I was in recovery
Or in their words, remission
But with the scans, once again
I needed confirmation of the truth

The words were coming in
I knew it was good news
I had seen these words before

Reading something is one thing
Hearing the words was another
The truth would be remission
I'm "lymphoma free" still

Relief went through me
But I knew it would rattle again
In the next six months or a few years

But it's better than the unknown
Especially when there's no preventive
Besides these scans to be aware
So I take good news when I can

HORROR PLANTS ::
BLOOD CANCER

What do they have in common?
Blood-sucking plants would connect
More with diabetes with the testing blood
Or even vampires, if they existed, taking blood

Blood cancer is like many horror plants
They take, and they take, without warning
Unless you're truly looking for it

It takes blood as food to digest
Each moment changes everything
Cancer can grow slow or fast
Plants can grow almost the same

Each takes a lot of power to destroy
It can take even people who aren't ready
If we work hard, we can find a way

Each of us can make a difference
As long as you're willing to learn
We can take cancer from horror
To obsolete diseases of the past

THE STUDIOUS GIRL

The one who tried to do her best
Everything she did, but would
Always feel like it is never enough

Was she trying to please others?
Or did she want to learn more?
Maybe it was a bit of both

Once she's taken from school
This Studious Girl kept going
Even at work, she doesn't feel
Good enough, no matter what

The demands are similar to others
But for you, they come harder
The fight against lymphoma
Changed this Studious Girl

Even she studies outside of work
So she is prepared for what's ahead
Improving her craft that she enjoys
She drains quickly each day

The world brings her unnecessary stress
If she could just focus on her joyful craft
Who would she be? Studious still?

STUCK IN LOOP REFLECTION

It would be the longest night
The loop would begin that night
Midnight was the nightmare
Of the chemo sleepless nights

The loop would—begin that night—
She never expected her mind's attention
Of the "Chemo Sleepless" nights
The repetition of unconscious thoughts

She never expected, her mind's attention
Would take her to a hospital bed
Midnight was the nightmare
Of the repetition of unconscious—
Thoughts—it would be the longest night

DANCING HERITAGE

I can hear the Greek music
It's calling me to dance
Did I belong within?
I wish I knew the steps
I wish I knew the words

I could see others dance
As they had learned
They belonged together
They knew the steps
They knew the words

Yet the notes seem to be
Flowing through me
The roots know more
Then what I wasn't taught
If only I had learned from
The ones in the past

The dance for heritage
Keeps going on in ways
No one can define within
It would take time for its flow
Deep down in the heart
The healing has started

LYMPHOMA AWARENESS

Chronic extreme fatigue for ages
Nothing seemed to explain it
Iron deficiency was found
But it wasn't the cause

A little swelling in the past
But one test didn't show enough
There would need to be a lot more
Swelling in the neck, the lymph nodes

A blood cancer, but hard to detect
Even with multiple blood tests
Beware of the side effects
Loss of appetite, night sweats

Recurring illnesses stood out
But the fatigue affected more
One might think it's just stress
Nothing quite like it can be

Even after fighting the fight
The extreme fatigue continues
How can you tell when your body
Has truly recovered? No one knows.

UNIQUE PLANTS, HERITAGE ROOTS

We're all unique plants, but some connect to
Our heritage roots matter more than anything
It's the connection to the past deep within

Some unique plants take time to grow
Just as healing from an infection or disease
If they can survive, it makes them stronger

Not the typical strength of a sturdy build
It's something that keeps the plant going
It isn't easy, but sometimes worth the price

Heritage roots have to be watered and cared for
Especially when it's a privilege to know
Sunlight on what needs to improve

We have the power to use our uniqueness
Just like our heritage roots for positive impact
If we don't, we lose more than you can imagine

THE POWER OF HEALING

She is still healing and she knows it
She doesn't know when it will happen
All she can do is hope it will come soon

She is held back by words told to her
The words that she cannot let go of
No matter how much she tries to
She won't let anything get in her way

She does what she always wants
When she knows what she wants
But some things stop her actions
Especially those out of her control

She wants to be a Greek goddess
Her power to make everything better
With the wisdom to know the best
Her mind and body capable of
Knowledge and Creativity always
Along with Compassion for others

It isn't as easy as a wave of a wand
Everything takes time, but how much
Will it take, how fast, and how slow?

The power of healing is in reach
As long as she takes time to rest
Care will be provided in all her steps

LET YOUR TEAM HELP

While you heal, it's only your body
It does the most work to repair
But besides your actions,
Others are there to help you

Those who find out what's wrong
Those who find the right treatment
Those who provide the treatment
Those who stay beside you always
Those who come to your aid

They are the team that is ready
For your healing journey to start
Guide you all the way through
Until the very end of the line

Don't fight to be independent
It will only make things harder
It's tough to do, I know it is
Especially when it's all you know

While there are things you can do
On your own can feel lonely
Find those who want to be
In the future as you

The words can be elusive
Especially if you are concerned
That no one will be able to afford
Time by your side when needed

You've lost a lot in the past
You might fear losing even more
Especially those who matter most
If they matter, they'll be there

Even if it isn't exactly how you hoped
Or even better than you imagined
It's time to be thankful for the team
That helped you get through

Even if it feels hard to do
It's as if everyone has gone
Busy days and no lack of care
So many people to speak to

Your healing journey is still going
Even months after treatment
It isn't seen, but they can hear
The words that remind them

Your team is still there waiting
You have to remind yourself
Don't be fooled by your fears
Your hope is stronger than eve

MY GRANDMA'S PEARLS

I'll always remember her pearls
She wore them for formal occasions
They became an aspect of who she was

Pearls come from oysters in the sea
Would it make sense that she would love
Someone who enjoyed having oysters

She never wanted to have oysters
She expected me to dislike them
But I enjoyed them and still do

I wear pearls thinking of her
They made me believe in beauty
Something she always wanted to be

Heartbroken young when beauty
Was taken away from her mother
Her father decided to leave them

Later she found a love that would last
One that would never abandon
Unless life took the decision instead

The pain would find her once again
In a disease that would break her down
Change her forever before her soul left

No matter what happens in life
I'll always remember her presence in pearls

WRITING STORMS AHEAD

She is on the beach waiting for something
If you looked at the distance, you would see
That gray clouds were sweeping across

She wasn't going to leave, she needed this
She standing tall beside the deck side
There are rocking chairs nearby ignored

If things were easy, she would be writing
The clouds were coming closer darker
Even the lightning and thunder knew too

She didn't leave even when the rain came
She just kept looking at the strong waves
They would have pulled her away from here

The rain was coming down stronger
She couldn't move from where she was
It didn't make sense to her, but we could

The storms were brewing through the mind
The lightning and thunder were her emotions
The hard rain was what she couldn't control

THE GREAT ROMANTIC

Something at the distance across
Needed his presence, he wouldn't leave
Standing tall with his hands in his pockets
Everything and everyone else ignored

If things were easy, he would be there
There was something dark taking hold
Even the night sky knew something too

She would leave when times were tough
He still kept looking at her with wonder
They would have gone away from here

The pool was full of summer water
She couldn't move from where she was
When he fell all because of her

It was going through her mind
The great romantic tore her emotions
The life she had she couldn't control

THE NEW ROARING TWENTIES

We expected fireworks for the new twenties
But it was like the previous one
Where we celebrated a lot and badly followed

As we recover, it still feels like we haven't learned
No matter what the numbers show in evidence
We are broken up into different groups

Some might still be hopeful as they should
As its the only way to keep striving forward
We celebrate the good among the threads

When we write history, what will we see?
The hardships of workers striking for fair deals
Women gather together to support each other

Will we be enough for the future generations?
Or will we be questioned for all our actions?
Our legacy is being written right now

HER THIRTIES AWAKENING

She never would have predicted her thirties
Be filled with unexpected illness, including hers
She rang her thirtieth birthday with a trip
For an incredible and unforgettable experience
After, the city was destroyed by a pandemic
She was diagnosed with an unexpected cancer

Just like her now, the city's in recovery mode
Just like her city, there's an awakening
To find a way forward any possible
It seems the same, but everyone is changed
She knows that she is different than before
She wants to make changes to her words

No matter what she wants, it seems out of reach
No matter what she tries to do, recovery is slow
She has a desire to live life fully, but she fears
Too much of everything will bring illness again
Where does she go? What life is she truly living?

LOVE OR WEALTH?

After illness, the answer is easy
But doesn't everyone want love
Not everyone would admit wealth
Neither is truly easy to come by

As well as it's difficult to keep
If you care, you'll find a way
Even then it's still never enough
When you're always pondering ahead

If you have love, you fear losing it
If you have wealth, you'll never keep it
Why do we have to choose between them?
We can never have enough real love
But we can have too much wealth

If you don't know how to truly use it
Wealth will not make you worthy
If you use it to support others
You find more value just like love
Nothing is more valuable than love
Recovery from illness comes close

FLASHBACKS

It seems like a typical sickness
What would a sore throat do?
To others, it might seem normal

Is it a typical sickness or allergy?
Or could it be something else?

It becomes flashbacks to the recent
Moments of the past with reoccurring
Illnesses that shifted into swelling
Until the news of lymphoma

Or the moments after treatments
Where the throat pain was unbearable
The fear of lymphoma looms,
But the fear of any pain
Seems minor in comparison
To everything that has happened

Minor to what violence occurs
Far away from here, but affects us
Minor to what the planet has become
Nature destroyed and limited resources

Not even words are enough
Everyone has a narrative
Which one is the right one?
From physical pain to anxiety
The flashbacks add to it all

THE SCAR WON'T HEAL

I see this scar every time
I take a shower each week
Every other time it's hidden
But when I do, I'm reminded

When I started my fight
With lymphoma and continued
Even after all the treatments
It was looming over my mind
As something that would stay
To remind me of the pain

A sign that I can get through
What life can throw at me
But it upsets me because
It won't heal no matter what

It reminds me that it could return
I would have to fight lymphoma again
I barely could get through it before
If I don't heal, how will I get through
How will I live with all my responsibilities
Of present and coming in the future
All the passions that I want to do

What would happen if the scar
Disappeared, would it be as if it were
A far distance memory or nothing at all

TIME OF MERCURY RETROGRADE

It's time for inner reflection
What gains we've made
Where we can improve
Where are we heading?

It's on our minds now
Time to rest for recharge
Focus on what's around
It will be our inspiration

Creativity is on the corner
New plans for the new year
When the shadow of Mercury
Its retrograde leaves in the tide
The fortnight will bring us
What we need now

INDIE AUTHOR POET STRIVING

One who writes verse and prose
Strives to find a way to do so always
The mind can be unpredictable
Just as life can have plot twists

How does one make strides forward?
When things get in the way
When there's so much on the plate
When your health continues to struggle

Or maybe it's mostly in your mind
Maybe you can do more than possible
Maybe you can still rest in between
Maybe you can be successful

So what is truly holding you back?
Is it everything you don't know?
Is it everything you can't control?
What are you going to do about it?
You're the indie author poet striving

NEW YEAR CONSTELLATION

See that star bright in the night sky?
There on the horizon, second to the right
That's the one that will improve my writing

Now let's look to the left, and you can see the one
that will keep me on track with my publishing journey

The one in the middle directing to the west
That's the one that keep me reading,
but most of all, enjoying what life is giving

TIME CHANGES

Winter, Spring, Summer, and Fall
It's the journey that I'll never forget
Winter began the fight against lymphoma
Hades tried to pull me under to his world

Spring held what Persephone's mother
Calls for renewal through good news
The fight against lymphoma would lead
Recovery soon after, but it would take

Through Summer and Fall to make sure
That healing process continued, but it's still
A journey that will continue for years

TIME CAPSTONE

If you graduated with piece of time
Would you pick a time when you fought
The hard fight of surviving cancer?

It seems like it would be the grade
That seems almost impossible to achieve
Would that look selfish to those who couldn't?

But we're thankful to even ponder it
Because some will never have enough
Time to really experience everything

How can you complete a year when
You know that anything can happen
Time can never be capped, but we can

So we can only be thankful for the time

NEXT CHAPTER

Where will we go from here?
It feels like an empty new journal
The start of the new year, new chapter

I don't know what is ahead, but ready
For the next adventure because the last
Was a struggle and I need more fun

When does recovery end in this journey?
I wish we could have the answer to this
But I want to fill the next with words

ODE TO READERS

You have made me an author
You have learned of my story
You continue to be inspired
Especially my lymphoma fight
You connect to my heritages
You support my passions
From writing and beyond
You follow my journey
You have read my stories

You have made me a poet
You inspire me to be me
While caring about myself
With multiple languages
You find yourself with me
You find me within my words

It hasn't been easy to start
You have been there to help
It's been difficult to get traction
You have still shown your worth
With your words and actions
Even though my hardest times
Thank you for being part of it all
This ode is always for you

IS IT OVER YET?

The question looms in mind
No matter the fact that time passes
It still feels like it's back to then
The moment of receiving diagnosis,
The months of tests and treatments,
The swift changes out of control

But the changes were even before
But no one knew what was within
Even though the body didn't feel right
No one could explain it until later
But thankfully it wasn't too late
For the toughest fight of all

While it should be noted that
Everything is now clear in scans
Recovery continues to be long
The concern of recurrence tightens
Among the longtime-rooted anxiety
And writing words takes more time

The question looms in mind
Is it over yet? Time will always tell

*This poem featured in Shelby Leigh's Poetry Club
Annual Magazine Issue December 2022:
'The Other Side of Pain' (download available
for free through Shelby's website or my website)*

NOVELLA-IN-VERSE:
PERFECT STORM

IT IS ME, REYNA TORRENTE

The start of the summer of my final year
In grad school, I received a call from mi tio
He needed me to stay at his beach house
I wouldn't have to head two hours home
Everything was packed and ready to go

A short car ride from the university island
To his beach house on Mustang Island
The city of Corpus Christi was a small
In comparison to other Texas cities
Known for the Tejano Queen Selena

There's not much I expect caring for a house
But mi mami taught me how every day
She would miss me when I don't return
But she knows I'll call her every day
Mi papi expects me to be independent

This will show him that I can
Everything will be fine as I spend time
Viewing the beach skyline with a book in hand
When everything inside is clean and ready
As I arrive, I worry it won't be as easy

WHEN I MET ANDER BRONTES

I was clearing the yard in front
He must have thought I was the help
The grass had grown as if no one cared
Mi tio left everything like huracán

Ander acted like we casually met at the mall
I couldn't find words, like meeting a star
He had the conversation in his control

He had left the school campus early
Learning online so he could carefully
Check on his lymphoma-affected mother

He said that staying by the beach
Was best, but his father wasn't there
Storm clouds were coming in his eyes

SUMMERTIME BEGINS

In the quiet of the morning,
I found the beach ready for me
No one was around by the shore
Seagulls were roaming the waves
Nature growing on the dunes

No one could bother me until
I noticed Ander at his house's porch
He was guiding his mom to a chair
Even from here, she looked fragile
He told me she was fighting lymphoma

I didn't know what that was
I knew from his face, that something serious
As soon as I could I rushed to search
Because he was the only one near my age
Besides his mom, he was all alone
I couldn't understand why

His father was out of the picture
Even though I know some marriages
Don't seem to last as they should
I could only hope that the beach would
Lead to Ander's mother's healing
Although she could only be seen
Outside in the morning and evening

Every step in this place gave me
Rejuvenated energy after a semester

MEETING HIS MADRE

She had a stare that almost went through me
I arrived on their porch with empanadas
I held to the plate tight like they were going
Fly away unexpectedly in the ocean breeze

Just her and I frozen in our designated spots
Ander didn't seem to be around to welcome
I couldn't think of a word to say to his mami
I didn't know how long I stood there waiting

Eventually, she told me, "He isn't here, hija."
The words spooked me at first but then I knew
"It's okay. These empanadas are for both of you."
She gave me a look. Then she took the plate.

"Take care of him, hija. That's all I want."
I wasn't sure what she was asking about.
"I will. Is there anything you may need?"
"Don't worry about me, hija." She went.

OUR FIRST DATE

Some would say that having your first date
With his mom would be a bad idea
But what could I do or say when
His mother needed her son
She was fighting lymphoma

He had the barbecue pit going
As we all sat outside watching it
Along with the waves rolling in
Not too much wind to change
He looked at me while silence
Filled the air of wide open space

It was easier to go with the flow
Just allow the silence to come
Even though I wanted to know
Everything about Ander and
Let him ask about me, isn't it
What is a first date all about?

Dating never came easy
It always seemed easier to
Stick with focusing on studying
We had some small talk
The classes we left behind
A bit of his mami's health
I knew they didn't want my pity
But should it be easier? Or were we just neighbors?

WEATHER ANNOUNCEMENT

I heard the news announcer say
"There's a hurricane on the way.
Prepare yourselves for the storm
If you're about to stay, but its best
To leave as soon as you can if you
Live near the South Texas coast

The waves will be stronger than
An average coastal day quickly
The winds will take on the roofs
The risk of tornados will be high
But if you want to stay, make sure
You find a way to board everything

Your lives will be on the line
We don't know if we will be able
To reach you in time, so make sure
You're ready today. We'll continue to
Provide you up to the minute updates."
All I could think of was, what will we do
We couldn't leave and we couldn't stay

WHAT ARE WE DOING?

I never did this, especially on my own
He insists that we can be storm-ready
Once he finishes with their house then
He will help me with mi tio's house

He slipped away as I stood there
I knew time was slipping by for us
Not just the storm coming our way
I barely knew him, but could I trust

That this would work out for us
I didn't even know my path in life
He has enough to deal with, let's add
Everything that I didn't know I could do

I wanted to know him, so I could trust
That all of this would work out for us

GETTING STORM READY

I could stare at him right now
I know it's just him doing what
Everyone else is doing to get ready
For the upcoming storm heading here

There's just a way about him
Easy-going, happy to help,
Is he doing it for me
Or because he feels like it?
Does it matter? I'm his assistant
For any tool or item that he needs
I carefully place boards on windows
I tie down where he suggests
I put things that need to be stored
I'll be locking everything up

He picked up food for three
I'll be staying with him
And his mom for free
No need to worry about it
He insists that it will be best
I walk away from mi tio's house
Wondering if everything will be

STAYING AT HIS HOUSE

Walking around with hesitancy
It was like not wanting to break
Crystals built as a beach house
I felt as a stranger breaking in

I don't know what to do with myself
Or the bags that I bought with me
What room could be mine tonight?
He suggests that I stay in his room

He'll be on the sofa, as his mami sternly
Nods to provide her hijo's approval
I'm left to my own devices to settle in
As he guides his mami in nightly routine

Settling into his bed felt familiar
Like night in family vacation
Yet so strange as the house creaks
The storm coming into the shore

MOMENT WITH HIM

All I want is a moment with him
Is that selfish of me to say right now?
The darkness swept around the house
I am sure everyone is asleep

So why am I hearing the storm
Having such a desire to be by his
Is it because I am scare of the house
Is he the blanket that will protect me

I close my eyes with hope it goes
Nothing seems to change as the dark
Leads into the eye lids in my mind
He stands there waiting to have a dance

THE STORM ARRIVES

I expected my arrival to be like a movie
Everyone ready to enjoy the night huddled
We would have dinner and listen to music
Some how we would find ourselves near

The storm wouldn't bother us at all
We would enjoy chatting with one another
We would find games to play as the storm
Raged on behind us as unexpected soundtrack

It arrived with a bang and shook the house
The wind swept up the rain onto the sides
Of where the house stood on unsteady sand
The power turned everything off along with
Any potential fun to be had this night fall

What could we do when one was struggling
With side effects of the worse diease imagined
What could I enjoy when it was his mother
What did it matter when I barely knew them

CONCERN FOR HIS MAMI

I woke up to sounds and darkness
If I was en mi casa I would sleep
Assured that mis padres would be
Getting ready early to start the day

I was somewhere else with wonder
Should I go find out or stay in bed?
What if his mami needed something?
Would he want me to help them?

My curiosity took over my mind
My body began to get out of bed
My feet heading towards the door
Walking as out of my control

Once I arrived, there he was standing
Beside his mami's bedside asking
What he could do to help subdue
The chemo symptoms she had still

Would they need to go to the hospital?
It wouldn't be safe to travel by car
The storm would have made a mess
Of the Texas roads, so how would we

I could see his concern and felt it too
The concern for his mami

YOU DON'T UNDERSTAND

Maybe we got lost in translation
I asked if there was anything I could do
He told me to leave and I didn't understand
Leave the room or his house

I said that I wanted to help them
He said that you can't understand
But how could I when he won't even
Let me know what's going on

He rushed out of the room
Maybe I shouldn't have followed
I didn't know what I said but
He said you don't understand

Let me understand his POV
Or was it his mami's illness
Or was she not recovering?
Even his hand through his hair
I couldn't help thinking that
He was handsome as he pushed
Me away from his side

GOING SLEEP UPSET

I feel like nothing I do is good enough
Why am I here anyway in this house?
I know they invited me, but don't feel it
I can't see what is happening outside

I shouldn't care, they don't know me
I don't know them enough either
Yet his shouts still ring in my ears
He's going through a lot, it shouldn't be

Yet I'm still crying unexpectedly
I'm tired, I'm sensitive, it's just that
Either way, I still care about them
I still care enough about what they do

Here I am walking through the house
How can I sleep with the storm outside
My heart storming deep within me
No matter what I'm going asleep upset

ENDLESS STORM

I lay in bed hearing the rain hit
Will this endless storm last all night?
I want to leave and I want to stay
No matter what I have to stay

The wind makes everything creak
Will those boards on the window stay
Or will it break like it feels within me
I used to love the storms, what changed?

Could it be the boy who caught my heart?
I want to imagine us holding each other
As the lighting brightens the night sky
But I'm alone and afraid of losing him

He's someone I want or want to save?
This endless storm that has me confused
I can't even think, but I can't sleep either
When will this endless storm end?

STORM CLEARS?

Light begins to appear through my eyes
It doesn't make sense to the darkness
That was wrapping around me hours ago
I look to the window of the room to see

It is clear of the storm boards we placed
It doesn't make sense… is this a dream?
Where am I? Oh, that's right, his place
Ander, I need to look for him

I rush out of the room into the kitchen
And I look around at areas of the house
It looks cleared of anyone around
Even though all the things stayed

Where did they go? What happened?
Will I be able to find them?
Will his mother be okay?
Will Ander be okay with me?

CAN I FIND HIM?

Why do I feel like I'm pulled out
Into the deep end by a strong current
I've looked all over for them to be gone
There's no note to be found or anything

Did I miss something? Could it be hiding?
Mi mami always said that we couldn't notice
What we are looking for when we're stressed
I wouldn't believe that a storm came through

If I had not looked outside and seen the wind
Damage throw tree limbs all over nearby homes
There were strange debris scattered around
Even with all that, the house looked calm

Why would they leave without telling me?
Did something happen to them? Or was I wrong?
Is there any way I could find them soon?
A phone tone rang out, like my mind,
Can I find him? Can they be found?

HIS MAMI IS WHERE?

As I moved around the house to find
The phone that was ringing somewhere
I knew it was one that belonged to the house
The one that stood there for years waiting

I finally pick up the phone to hear the call
My mind froze, what would I say, it's not mine
A young female voice spoke, it's unknown to me
"We're calling to inform you about Mrs…"

They were calling for who? I don't want to know
I don't know what I could even say about them
"He told me to call because he doesn't want to leave"
Leave? He already left… or maybe he never been

"Are you there? Do you need me to repeat?"
Was I there? I couldn't understand her words
Did I need the repetition? I wasn't even sure
I ask her, "His mami is where?"

She said, "She is at the hospital."

NEW PATH

He sat by her side just as I was told
I didn't need to know anything
Somehow I understood that
Something was wrong

He looked up at me
I tried to hold onto my breath
As if I was diving within the ocean
But I was waiting to see what he said

"I woke up this morning with determination
I would remove all the boards for the storm
When I got back inside, mi mami looked unwell
I didn't know what to do, but to call for help…"

"Why didn't you tell me what was wrong?"
"I couldn't. I don't have any excuses."
"Is she going to be okay? What's wrong?"
"All I know is that she is better now."

"What does that mean? Is she cured?"
"She is still recovering, but getting better."
"What do you want me to do to help?"
"There isn't anything you can do."

"I feel helpless to all of this."
"You don't have to stay."
"You want me to leave?"
"It would be easier for you."

I wanted to stay to be with him
I wanted to leave, I didn't want pain
Did he really want me to stay here

Did he really want to know me?
Or was it time for a new path?

ACKNOWLEDGEMENTS

Thank you to everyone who has supported my indie author career and helped improve every aspect of my publishing journey. I'm also thankful for the support I received during my fight with lymphoma, especially from the writing community (including Paula Yoo, MJ Golias, Callie Thomas, Christina Farley, Beth Revis, Racquel Henry, May Leonardo, R.L. Medina, Priscilla Oliveras, Angelina M. Lopez, Megan Dawn Jones, and many more), but also from my friends (including Jennifer Lyn), family, co-workers, and those who inspire me. I wouldn't be able to continue to my indie author career.

I want to thank all those who have taught me to be a better writer, including as a poet throughout the years. Most recently Shelby Leigh (who is also a poet) has taught me about poetry and provided me amazing opportunities to learn and grow through her poetry club. She has also taught me knowledge about publishing and marketing my books through her creatives' content club. She is one of many who has made this book and a lot of what I do possible. I also want to thank Cristina Yun Lee for her support and knowledge about marketing with a storytelling focus in mind. She has helped me focus on the qualities that help me stand out.

ABOUT THE AUTHOR

Christina Vourcos

Christina Vourcos writes what matters from Latinx Romance to a range of poetry. As a Greek Latina, she is inspired by both of her cultures, and aims to represent her Latinx heritage, which isn't focused on in many mediums. She enjoys making nerd references in her writing. Christina fought lymphoma in 2022-2023. While in remission, she aims to advocate for everyone affected by blood cancer or any cancer.

BOOKS BY THIS AUTHOR

Write From The Heart, Edit With Precise Measure: A Poetry & Short Story Collection

Writing Matters And So Do You: Writing With A Mental Health Focus

Liberty Calling: Latinx Romance Novel

Never Forget: Latinx Scifi Mystery College Romance Novel

Starlight Holidays (Coming Soon)

Untitled Poetry Book (Coming Soon)

Made in the USA
Las Vegas, NV
09 July 2025